Love In Action

Encountering Gods manifold dimension of healing and power through intimacy

Alexander Emoghene

Love In Action

Encountering Gods manifold dimension of healing and power through intimacy

Tulip Publications

Ceintuurbaan 23b

3051AG

Rotterdam

Web: Tulippublications.com

Claypotchurchint.com

ISBN: 978-90-828720-1-9

Cover Design & Page Layout By: www.wearereach.org

Endorsements

In an age marked by the never-ending quest for something new, Pastor Alex has stepped back into the stream of foundational Christen teaching, bringing forth life-changing truths contained in the doctrines of righteousness and holiness. However, don't be put off by the idea of reading a book of dry doctrine- far from it, for from start to finish, the emphasis is placed not only on understanding but also on taking practical steps to enjoy the benefits of righteousness and holiness. Pastor Alex's approach reminds us that the teachings of the Scriptures are intended to change lives, and therefore of particular value are the suggested prayer response at the end of each section. This short but inspiring devotional should certainly remind us of the abundant provision our Father God has made to ensure that we can live a life of victory in our Lord Jesus Christ in this life with the assurance that the best is yet to come.

Pastor Karl Dennis
Kingdom Central
Birmingham UK

In his book Love in Action, Alexander Emoghene has meticulously disclosed and unleashed the most awesome revelation of how to live in righteousness within the Kingdom of God. His fresh, innovative and masterful approach to the different subjects on real love, holiness, and how to be in the presence of God daily will leave you with an overwhelming and exciting expectancy to read this devotional on daily basis.

Love in action gives you keys to walk in overcoming power in such a time as this. Alexander has birthed out this book out of his own life, he is part of that remnant who has completely given his life for the building and establishing of Gods Kingdom.

Out of his deep compassion for people and a deep passion for the Lord, he will take you on a journey in finding your true identity in your role as a Royal Priesthood, being a holy nation and how to use all the resource made available for us.

This is a book of action. I have confidence that it will greatly impact your life, a must read for every leader and believer in this day.

Apostle Paullette Boschmans Forbes
Powerhouse ministries
Eindhoven, The Netherlands

This devotional has the dept and illustrations to build, challenge, and encourage believers in all aspects of life. It is truly a daily devotional book that will minister to souls and deal with all aspects of the emotions through the help of the Holy spirit.

Once again Pastor you have break barriers and stethoscopes of putting this together once again congratulations. Areas highlighted in red may need to look into ..Well done sir

Emmanuel Boye Oluwasanya
Resident Pastor @ KICC Ilford Chapel. UK

Preface

There are many elements in this life that pose as major distractions from faith in God through Jesus Christ. However, once an individual is set to follow the way, there is no stopping them. I wrote this book because there is no better place to start a walk of faith, and continue in it, than to understand the force of the righteousness and the holiness of God. Even though this may seem to be old doctrine I have set to highlight the practicalities and make it applicable to the reader.

The subtitle of this book is encountering Gods manifold dimensions of healing and power through intimacy, by meditating on the content of this book you will be enlightened with fresh grace and empowered to live a life of intimacy with God. Your personal contact with the Father strengthens as you repeatedly spend time with Him and meditate on His righteousness and holiness toward you.

The simplicity involved is truly inspired by the Lord. It is a heartfelt book that will engage your spirit to draw closer to the Lord without fear or hesitation. It endeavours to help, cultivate the spirit of boldness in your walk of faith. Also, it will help you draw near to Gods plans for you while at the same time empowers you to engage in your divine assignment with real assurance of God's helping presence.

I believe it will bring healing on many levels to the reader, like in areas of doubt, embarrassment and low self-esteem. The devotional will tackle the negative side of the spirit of performance, help victims of verbal abuse, teach you how to battle negative thoughts concerning your faith and deal with issues of acceptance and much more.

From the moment that the Lord placed this topic on my heart, my personal worship and times of fellowship with Him soared to new heights. Prayer has become more of a delight and my fellowship with the Holy Spirit is growing to new heights daily. So, I urge you to join me and commit to making this a 40-day journey to greater intimacy with the Lord!

Alexander Emoghene

Prayer of Faith

After all is said and done, the goodness of God is here to lead us to the saving knowledge of God through Jesus Christ. Your journey in righteousness and holiness begins with your decision to accept and receive Jesus Christ as your Lord and Saviour.

2 Corinthians 5:22: For God made Christ, who never sinned, to be the offering for our sin, so that we could be made right with God through Christ. - NLT

For this journey to even begin, one must first be made right with God by receiving Jesus as Lord. You must be willing to admit that you cannot be righteous with your efforts, but only through the free-gift that has been giving in Jesus Christ.

Roman 5:17: For the sin of this one man, Adam, caused death to rule over many. But even greater is God's wonderful grace and his gift of righteousness, for all who receive it will live in triumph over sin and death through this one man, Jesus Christ.

Pray this from your heart: - Lord Jesus, thank you for your sacrifice for me, I receive you as my Lord and Saviour. From henceforth, I repent of all my sin and I live my life for you. I am born again, I am now the righteousness of God by faith in Christ Jesus.

Congratulations, as you have prayed this prayer your journey in Gods righteousness has just begun!

Philippians 2:13 (AMPC)
(Not in your own strength) for it is God Who is all the while effectu-
ally at work in you (energizing and creating in you the power and
desire), both to will and to work for His good pleasure and satisfac-
tion and deligh

Table of Contents:

Introduction

This book is not a comparison between righteousness and holiness. Instead, these words are intended to show our link to the divine God, who has opened wide the gates for us to enter boldly and have fellowship and friendship with Him in LOVE.

Why love? Because God is love[1] and all of His ways are motivated by love. The apostle Paul showed us a better way when he wrote, *"And now abide in faith, hope, love, these three; but the greatest is love."*[2]

Now, this love Paul mentions here is called *agape* in the Greek; it is unconditional love. This love can only be known and experienced by having a direct relationship with God, because no man can render this kind and quality of love.

The key word that you will come across in this book is love. The Bible confirms God's motives:

According as He hath chosen us in Him before the foundation of the world that we be holy and without blame before Him in **Love.**[3]

When it comes to human beings, whom God made in His likeness[4], He is motivated by love. The scripture says, *"For God so loved the world that He sent his only begotten Son that whoever believes in Him should not perish but have everlasting life[5]."* Love is His motive for redeeming man from sin. Again, we read in the book of Romans: *"But <u>God</u> demonstrated His own <u>Love</u> toward us,*

---

1   1 John 4:8

2   1 Corinthians.13:13

3   Ephesians 1:4

4   Genesis 1:26

5   John 3:16

in that while we were <u>yet sinners</u>, Christ died for us."[6] The amplified version of the Bible states, *"But God shows and clearly proved His [own]* **love** *for us by the fact that while we were still sinners Christ [the Messiah, the anointed one] died for us."*

Therefore, God urges all people to be motivated by that same love with which He has loved us. We should stand aloof from rituals, traditions, and religious ordinances. In His day here on earth, Jesus was against the teachers of the Law; he said, *"Thus you have made the commandment of God of no effect by your tradition."*[7]

In addition, Jesus said, *"If anyone loves me, he will keep my words; and My father will Love him, and we will come unto him, and make our abode with him."*[8] He went on to say, *"He who does not Love Me does not keep my word; and the word which you hear is not mine but the father's who sent me."*[9] But before these words, Jesus said, *"If you Love Me keep my commandment."*[10]

In essence, our service for and towards Him must be motivated by love in everything, or else we would walk in religion and monotony of works. This will lead to burnout and defeat.

The love Jesus uses here is the God kind of love. As you'll recall, in the Greek it is called *agape*, meaning 'the ability to love unconditionally.' Jesus is saying, in effect, "You have received the unconditional love from me. Now if you can come to me in the same unconditional attitude in love, which I have, and have shown you, by coming downward to reach and save you. Now you have the ability to keep my commandments in love."

In striving to uphold God's commandments, a lot of us Christians have formed ways, traditions, and religions to try to reach the standard set by Christ's holiness, when really we should be loving Him in a relational way as our brother, friend, and Lord.

This book will speak plainly of what Holiness really is and what righteousness is in the life of a child of God. At the end of each section is a prayer that draws upon the ideas discussed in that section.

---

6 Romans 5:8
7 Matthew 15:6
8 John 14:23
9 John 14:24
10 John 14:15

Use these prayers in your daily life to help you communicate with God and enrich your bond with the Lord by building a close relationship with Him.

Holiness

Holiness in itself is not being set apart, but the process of acting out the result and the quality of having been already set apart. It's a state of being called sanctification; in the Greek it is called *hagaismos*, meaning 'set apart,' or 'separated.'

Holiness is the process whereby the continuous use of the word of God exercises our senses so much that we can discern between good and evil.[11]

In my view, sanctification therefore is God, who literally took us away from the darkness of the world and into the marvellous light of His Son[12], and then poured His life into us in full measure and went on to pour out His life into us which is full of love, in full power, in full purity, in full peace, and in full joy. Sanctification is many things pertaining to His light, which is Christ in us the Hope of Glory.[13]

Sanctification is not a process; it is a done deal. In the words of Jesus, "It is finished." Sanctification speaks of a finished work, signed with the blood of the lamb, glory to His holy name.

HOLINESS IS THIS SIGNED DOCUMENT IN ACTION–LOVE IN ACTION.

The apostle Peter related this process of sanctification and holiness when he wrote the pilgrims who were scattered around early Europe. He said, *"Elect according to the foreknowledge of God the Father, in <u>sanctification of the Spirit</u>, for <u>Obedience</u> and <u>the sprinkling of the blood</u> of Jesus Christ."*[14]

---

11   Hebrews 5:13–14
12   Colossians 1:13
13   Colossians 1:27
14   1 Peter 1:2

John wrote that if we walk in the light, we have fellowship with one another, and the blood of Jesus Christ cleanses us from sin.[15]

This light talks about His sanctification, where walking in obedience as in the light shows the process and the force of holiness. The blood speaks of our cleansed life, as guaranteed by the shed blood of Jesus.

Therefore, the rate at which you are able to become aware of what God has already done in you will determine the ratio of the force of God you are able to release here on earth.

Righteousness

Righteousness can be termed as the legal framework provided by God in favour of man to enter into fellowship with Him without a sense of sin or guilt.

Therefore, righteousness is the jurisdictional power handed over to man by God to punish the power and the product of sin and all works of the devil. This power is made available to all through the shed blood of our Lord and saviour Jesus Christ's sacrificial death and bodily resurrection.

With the righteousness of God, there are no variations. All of God's children been given the same righteousness, whether the saint that was born again today or the one that was born again twenty years ago.[16]

Therefore, it is this working power of righteousness that separates the believer from the rest of the world and empowers the believer to produce the actions and attitudes we refer to as holiness.

We do not forget that we enter in only by faith. Faith is what will enable you to receive revelation concerning holiness and righteousness. Faith in Jesus and faith in his blood is what enables us to enter into God's grace, be justified, and then be declared righteous by God[17] to receive his righteousness. The Bible says that without faith it is impossible to please God.[18] In Ephesians, Paul show us,

---

15   1 John 1:7
16   Romans 3:22
17   Romans 5:24–26
18   Hebrews 11:6

"For by grace are ye saved through Faith; and that not of yourselves: it is a gift of God."[19]

So God commands us to live holy because God is holy. This is not a ridiculous command for His private entertainment as He watches down on mankind who, at every turn, are trying to be holy and failing each time. Rather, it is a love command of God by which we can surely take charge of our circumstances instead of our circumstances taking charge of us, because he has put every strength and wisdom within us so that we can remain on top and win always.

This is the reason He has provided righteousness: to shield and protect you, to empower and develop you, to nurture and encourage you. He did not stop there—He provided the vehicle called faith, and you only must jump in and ride to meet with Him, believing He is able to make all grace abound to you, that you in all things have sufficiency, and that you may abound to every good work.[20]

---

19   Ephesians 2:8
20   2 Corinthians 9:8; Ephesians 2:10; 1 Peter 2:9

Holiness is the Attitude of Being, not Becoming

A car does not try to become a car; neither does a tree try to become a tree. It is a tree; it simply grows into one and it yields its fruits in due season.

When you accept Christ as your Lord and saviour, God pours His spirit into your spirit. Just like water being poured into a glass, He comes and fills you up with His spirit. His spirit is holy—after all, that is His name: the HOLY SPIRIT. Therefore, when you are saved, you are called a holy nation because you are now a partaker of God's divine nature. What does this mean? God is holy[21] and His spirit now resides in you. You can now exhibit holy attributes with ease. Holiness no longer becomes what you go out for; it is what comes out of you.

> *Holiness no longer becomes what you go out for; it is becomes what comes out of you*

"*…But you are a chosen generation, a royal priesthood, a HOLY nation, His own special people, that you may proclaim the praises of Him who called you out of darkness into His marvellous light.*"[22]

Furthermore, Peter described our advantages as being holy, when he declared us "*…a Holy Nation.*" By no means was he pointing out our assignment; rather, he was pointing out our

---

21   Leviticus 11:45
22   1 Peter 2:9 NKJV

enthronement. We have become HOLY, just as God is holy. We live out of a holy reservoir as we walk with Him.

Our content is holy; our breath is holy; we are a nation of holy people. You might want to say—in racial terms, that is—we are a holy race of people, a special holy race that has never existed before.

God is saying through His word that we are now sharers of His divine nature. As a result of your conversion to a relationship with Christ, God makes you a new creation.[23]

You see, your old creation struggled to keep a right balance between wrong and right, bad and good, and your conscience was always battling to reconcile these issues that seemed insurmountable. In contrast, your new nature is able to rest from all these. Your new nature carries around the mind of Christ[24] and the holy nature of God.[25] Therefore, your new nature can rightly divide and separate these thin lines of doubt and make them clear.

We have given up the old creation, which we became familiar with all those years—that old nature, so blind and ignorant, stubborn and proud, full of death and sin, that caused so much trouble and pain. Thank God we have exchanged that corruption for the incorruptible—a new nature that is of God. It is full of glory and peace, rich with joy unspeakable and rest beyond measure. We have goodness, mercy, love—so much love, and a guarantee of life with God after the earthly life.

Prayer: Dear Lord, thank You for pouring yourself into me. This day I receive Your righteousness which is in me. I walk in it today, Lord. I receive grace from You today, Lord, to effect changes in my life that will enable me to manifest more of Your love toward me.

---

23   2 Corinthians 5:17
24   1 Corinthians 2:16
25   2 Peter 1:4

Righteousness is God's Being

Righteousness is God's state of being, and being righteous displays this state.

Righteousness is God's jurisdictional power to judge, sentence, and make or set free a convict. This is what the sinner goes through for God to declare him or her righteous. Therefore, this jurisdictional power works in the favour of the sinner who is willing to be saved or believe in the gospel of righteousness. It is also for the saint to stand without having a sense of guilt when the enemy comes to accuse or to intimidate the believer's walk in the life.

The Bible declares, "*...the Lord executes righteousness and justice [not for me alone but] for all who are oppressed.*"[26] Sin is an oppressor, so when God's righteousness judges 'sin,' the burden will be lifted.

The same can be said of sickness. About Jesus the Bible says how God anointed Jesus with the Holy Spirit and power and He went about doing good and healing all those who were oppressed.[27]

> **Righteousness is God's divine state, power, and ability, which keeps and performs all God's promise without failing.**

Righteousness is of God. It came from God, and it is God's divine state, power, and ability, which keeps and performs all God's promises in the lives of the believer and the nonbeliever without failing.

---

26   Psalms 103:6 AMP
27   Acts 10:38

It is God's jurisdictional power to execute vengeance on the enemy. To pass judgement over sickness and disease by bringing healing, and to judge sin and bring forgiveness.

Righteousness is what God has now made the believer become. The scripture says that for our sake He made Christ (virtually) to be sin who knew no sin, so that in and through Him we might become (endued with, viewed as being in, and an example of) the righteousness of God (what we ought to be, approved and acceptable and in right relationship with Him, by His Goodness). We have been made the righteousness of God.[28]

So we have become an instrument in the hands of God to judge the devil and to establish the Kingdom of God here on earth. To heal the sick and to deliver those who are oppressed by the devil, to destroy the works of the devil, and to bring the good news of salvation to the world. It is the righteousness that does all that.

Prayer: Lord, I believe that You have chosen me to be Yours here on earth. I stand in agreement with Your Holy Spirit, to establish Your Kingdom here on earth. Thank You, Lord, for giving me the great privilege to be a part of what You are doing.

---

28   2 Corinthians 5:21 AMP

Holiness is a Longing Heart in Love to Please God

" As the heart pants and longs for the water brooks, so I pant and long for you, O God. My inner self thirsts for God, for the living God. When shall I come and behold the face of God."[29]

Holiness stems from within the inner man. It is not an exterior posture, but that cry from the inside of man to touch God in love that sometimes cannot be expressed.

> **Holiness stems from within the inner man, not an exterior posture**

This is an act of love being expressed voluntarily from deep within, knowing full well the presence of God and His great love that He has first poured into a believer's heart.[30]

Holiness is that automatic drive to God early in the morning, before the sun rises. King David said, *"My voice you shall hear in the morning. O Lord; in the morning I will direct it to you and I will look up."*[31]

Holiness in this one verse shows how King David moved his own will to praise God in the morning, in the privacy of his home, where nobody sees his performance. Jesus advises, *"But when you pray, go into your room, and when you shut your door, pray to your*

---

29 Psalms 42:1–2
30 Romans 5:5
31 Psalms 5:3

Father who is in the secret place; and your Father who sees in secret will reward you openly."[32]

Holiness is what Paul expressed in this prayer:

[For my determined purpose is] that I may know Him [that I may progressively become more deeply and intimately acquainted with Him, perceiving and recognising and understanding the wonders of His person more strongly and more clearly], and that I may in that same way come to know the power out flowing from His resurrection [which it exerts over believes], and that I may so share His suffering as to be continually transformed [in spirit into His likeness even] to His death [in the hope].[33]

Prayer: Lord, give me a thirst that comes from deep within my most inner being to know You, and may my trust in following You be more progressively and intimately deeper without reservation, and may my desire that flows from my innermost being be of truth.

32   Matthew 6:6
33   Philippians 3:10 AMP

Righteousness is God Who Pleased Us out of Love

Righteousness describes a God who took great pleasure in reaching humanity, bringing about salvation from the government of Satan. In the gospel of Luke, Jesus declares, *"Do not fear, little flock, for it is your Father's good pleasure to give us His Kingdom."*[34] This is the authority and power that brought His government.

Because of righteousness and the love to see mankind healed from every disease, pain, and grief, Jesus was bruised for us and it pleased the Lord. *"Yet it pleases the Lord to bruise Him; He has put Him to grief: when you make His soul an offering for sin, He shall see His seed days, and the pleasure of the LORD shall proper in His hand."*[35]

> **Righteousness shows a God with the loving heart to seek and save the lost.**

Again it says, *"In Him we have redemption (deliverance and salvation) through His blood, the remission (forgiveness) of our offenses (shortcomings and trespasses), in accordance with the riches and generosity of His gracious favour, which He lavished upon us in every kind of wisdom and understanding (practical insight and prudence). Making known to us the mystery (secrets) of His will (of His plan, of His purpose). [And it is this],* **In accordance**

34	Luke 12:32
35	Isaiah 53:10

with His good pleasure *(His merciful intentions) which He had previously purposed and set forth in Him."*[36]

Righteousness shows a God with the loving heart to seek and save the lost, to bring us into His presence, and to give us His power to live in there. Forgiveness and forgetfulness are the privilege of the righteousness of God.[37] It pleases God to see us share from the blessings in His presence. After all is said and done, the power of sin that was in our lives before we believed could not stop His righteousness from reaching us.

It is His righteousness that will pull the nations from far and near, to His saving grace.[38]

Prayer: Lord, by faith I receive joy today to worship You in every season of my life. By faith, Lord, I pray for Your anointing in my life, to overflow as I sit down to receive Your word in my meditations and prayers.

My Father, by faith I know that You have stored up great and mighty promises of spiritual might, wealth, and health for me; therefore, I receive the keys to Your storerooms and unlock these promises for my life today.

I receive divine wisdom and understanding in everything that I do today, to fulfil Your good pleasure here on earth.

I will walk therefore in this life in godliness because of Your provision, as Your virtue is being released daily in my life to walk in all excellence.

---

36   Ephesians 1:7–9 AMP
37   Psalms 103:12
38   Luke 13:29

Holiness is Love Towards God

How many of us would genuinely strive on a daily basis to be the best, so that someone somewhere may appreciate us in what we do? So many. Holiness, although an inward activity within the believer, would certainly flow outward, but this flow should not be directed to the accolades received from man; rather, it should billow upward to the throne room of God.

Holiness inquires for God at all times. It searches and longs for God's word always, as it yearns to do all the instruction. Jesus says, *"If you love Me keep My commandments (if you continue to obey My instruction), you will abide in My love and live on in it, just as I have obeyed My Father's commandments and live on in His love."*[39] Job declared, *"I have not departed from the commandment of His lips; I have treasured the words of His mouth; more than my necessary food."*[40]

Holiness is allowing the holy seed of God, which was imbued in the believer at the time of the new birth, to grow steady in the grace of God. John, the apostle of love, clarified that whoever is born of God does not sin, for His seed remains in him; and he cannot sin, because he has been born of God.41

Prayer: Lord, make me free indeed from the doubts and fears of this world. I declare my holy status in the name of Jesus Christ, my salvation. Let me experience the power and the force of Your holiness today, I pray.

---

39   John 15:10.
40   Job 23:12
41   1 John 3:9

Righteousness is God's Emanating Love for Us

Righteousness is God demonstrating His love for us towards us. It is commonly said about Jesus that it was not the nails that kept Him on the cross; it was the love He had for us.

Apostle Paul says, *"But God demonstrated His Love toward us, in that while we were yet sinners, Christ died for us."*[42]

John, the apostle of love, proclaimed, *"For God so LOVED the world that He sent His only begotten Son, that whosoever believed in Him should not perish but have everlasting life."*[43]

Therefore, righteousness is God reaching down by His own strength to save man from sin and death of all kind (including sickness, disease, oppression, depression, loneliness, and suicidal tendencies). In doing all this, He shows and pours down His love on mankind.

Often, I meditate on the scene in the Bible where Jesus was reaching down with His mighty saving hand to rescue Peter from the raging sea. It teaches me of the righteousness of God reaching down to pull us up from the raging seas of life. It might be the seas of debt, divorce, fear, doubts, confusion, depression, greed, or envy. In all cases it is His righteousness that moves to save.[44]

---

42   Romans 5:8
43   John 3:16
44   Zephaniah 3:17

Prayer: Father, I rejoice today as You rejoice over me. Thank You, for You are mighty to save. I dedicate this day to You from the depths of my heart for Your mighty saving grace.

Holiness is Giving God All Passion

Speaking about Jesus, the Bible says, *"The zeal of your house have eaten me up."*[45] Can you make such a confession from your heart? Passion can sometime be mistaken for fanaticism. Passion is coordinated anger in the face of agents of defiance. Passion speaks of great enthusiasm about one's belief system. Passion is true love in action.

Jesus showed all of this energy when it came to His Father's house. When He saw the mess that was going on in the temple, which was supposed to be a house of prayer, He did not stay still and passive but instead acted with passion.

Apostle Paul relayed to the church in Philippi how much zeal he had when he was not converted. *"Concerning zeal, he said persecuting the church."*[46] Well, he thought he was doing God service, until God saved him from sin. Now in his life in Christ, he gave a picture of having to work for God with more zeal when he wrote, *"Brethren, I do count myself to have apprehended; but one thing I do forgetting those things which are behind and reaching to those things are ahead, I press to the goal for the prize of the upward call of God in Christ Jesus."*[47]

How passionate are you about the things of God? Do you stand up for the word, when what you believe is challenged? The

---

45   John 2:17
46   Philippians 3:6
47   Philippians 3:13–14

Bible spoke of Apollos as one having a fervent spirit[48]; that same word is compared with zeal, as the Bible said he spoke boldly. Paul stood at one time for three months, reasoning and persuading concerning the things of the Kingdom of God.

Prayer: Lord, here I am today. Transform all timidity in me to boldness. My Lord, make me a voice and no longer an echo. Lord, I declare my boldness to express my desire for You today!

---

48 Acts 18:25

Righteousness is God's Passion Toward Us

God is very passionate toward His people; He loves us in a passionate way. He reassured the Israelites that He loved them with an everlasting love.[49] God's passion not to see man lost is what brought Jesus down to die for humanity. We even call His last hours on earth, on His way to the cross, His Passion.

The message of the cross is a passionate one. Jesus said, *"Greater love has no one than this, than to lay down one's life for His friends."*[50]

In the parable of the lost sheep, Jesus showed us the love and passion of the shepherd, when the shepherd abandoned the ninety-nine safe sheep in search of the one that was lost.[51] Again in the parable of what we now know as the lost son, the passionate father stood by the door looking at the horizon in wait for his son who'd decided to leave home. Jesus builds the story at the end, showing us a father who ran out passionately to greet the son and welcome his son with kisses.

Passion[52] is what depicts the symbols of the Holy Spirit. For example, the rushing mighty wind and the flame of fire are explosions of passion. When Peter was preaching a long sermon in Cor-

---

49 Jeremiah 31:3
50 John 15:13
51 Luke 15:6
52 Acts 2:1

nelius's house, the Holy Spirit could not wait for him to finish when He interrupted the flow of the meeting and filled the room with His presence.[53]

How high is your passion?

Prayer: Father, please increase my Passion for You today. Increase my Passion for lost humanity. Lord, I hunger for an outpouring of Your Holy Spirit in my life.

---

53   Acts 10:44

Holiness is Thinking About God

Never forget that holiness is a lifestyle, not just a conduct, a service or a worship service. Holiness is displaying what is inside to match what is seen outside. Holiness is answering to spiritual things and performing spiritual things. As it is written, *"Even when we were dead in trespasses, made us alive together with Christ (by grace you have been saved), and raised us up together, and made us sit in heavenly places in Christ Jesus."*[54]

If this is now our position, we should only set our minds therefore on spiritual things, in order to effect things in a more effective way.

The helmet of salvation the Bible encourages us to put on is said to be the most elegant armour of a Roman soldier. It is conspicuous, and it is worn with pride. How often do you think about your salvation, or has it become an ugly thing you wear? Do people look upon you and say, "Wow, how can I get that helmet that you are wearing?"

Paul drew our attention when he wrote, *"Those who live according to the flesh set their minds on the things of the flesh, but those who live according to the spirit, the things of the spirit."*[55] Paul went further to advise the Galatians when he said, "I say then, 'Walk in the spirit and you shall not fulfil the lust of the flesh.'"[56]

---

54   Ephesians 2:5–6
55   Romans 8:5
56   Galatians 5:16

Our minds need to be stayed in God at all times[57] and not waver. Then we can have peace and satisfaction. Paul also advised us to think about the pure things of God: His works in our lives and the lives of others.[58]

So do not let your heart go through a day without appreciating something that God has done, and it shall be well with you.

Prayer: Father, in Your righteousness, help me to guide my thought life. I commit to a daily meditation of Your holy word. My Father, I really want to become more familiar with Your thought life.

---

57   Isaiah 26:3
58   Philippians 4:8

Righteousness is
What God Thinks
About You

I heard this from somebody—I hope you are reading this book. He said that when God is speaking, He is speaking Jesus, and when he is thinking, He is thinking about us. I wish I was the originator of this statement because it really brings me to a place of worship when I meditate about it.

Truly the Bible says, *"What man that you are so mindful of him,"*[59] meaning God does not do anything without thinking of man, because the next line says, *"The son of man that you visit him."* In the event of creation, the Lord God said, *"Let us make man in our own Image and in our likeness."* This is God expressing His thought with the co-equal Godheads Jesus Christ and the Holy Spirit. In Hebrew the word *logos* actually means 'an expression of a thought.'

The same word is used in John 1:1 to reveal the entrance of God the son into earthly places: *"In the beginning was the word and the word was with God and the word was God."* This is an expression of a thought, which eventually becomes evident. Therefore, whatever God has thought about you must come into existence. Powerful!

God shared His thought with us through His prophet Jeremiah: *"I know the thoughts that I think toward you, says the Lord, thoughts of peace and not of evil, to give you a future and a hope."*[60]

---

59   Psalms 8:4a
60   Jeremiah 29:11

Do not be alarmed about what is going on right now. God's word concerning you will definitely come to pass and move you into the places where all your dreams will be fulfilled.

Prayer: Oh Lord, make me more patient so that I can truly see Your manifested thoughts for me in this life and the one to come. Somehow, I know that they are great thoughts because you are a great God. Thank You for Your thought towards me!

Holiness is Spoiling God with Gifts of Love

Make a joyful noise to the Lord, all you lands! Serve the Lord with gladness! Come sing before His presence with singing! Know (perceive, recognise, and understand with approval) that the Lord is God! It is He who made us, not we ourselves [and we are His]! We are His people and the sheep of His pasture. Enter his gates with thanksgiving and a thank offering and into his courts with praise! Be thankful and say so to Him, bless and affectionately praise His name. (Psalms 100:1-4)

The first offering that we should lavish on God is our bodies: *"I beseech you therefore brethren by the mercies of God that you present your bodies a living sacrifice, holy acceptable to God, which is your reasonable service."*[61] This gift is that of the service of love, where you are available to carry out the work of God with gladness. This kind of service is extremely fulfilling, and eventually very beneficial.

The second gift to be lavished on God is our time. The Bible is clear about spending time in the things of God. It also urges us on our daily preparedness about the things of God: *"Be instant in season and out of season"*[62]; this means speaking about your faith every opportune time. Jesus said, *"If any desire to follow me let him deny himself, and take up his cross daily and follow Me."*

The third gift is that of thankful praise at all times[63]. We need

---

61   Romans 12:1
62   Timothy 4:2
63   Psalms 34:1

to be praise tanks from which the Lord can draw at any moment. We must be ready to satisfy the Lord with the fruit our lips[64] when we think about Him and His goodness. "Make a joyful noise to the Lord, all you lands! Serve the Lord with gladness!"

The fourth gift is that we need to allow ourselves to be used as His hands and legs here on earth, to bless those we meet everyday and to cause somebody to smile because the Lord, through one of His ambassadors, has touched them[65]. In doing so we are spoiling God with the gift of love.

The fifth gift is in our giving to the work of God. People have issues with bringing gifts into the house of God, probably because they feel that the church is not worth so much blessing. That focus is wrong[66]; it is God all the while asking us to bring in a sacrifice of praise and gifts of all kinds.[67] During an offering season in the temple, the Bible says about Jesus, *"And He <u>looked up</u> and saw the rich putting their gifts into the treasure, and He saw also a certain poor widow putting in two mites."*[68]

This shows that Jesus saw the offerings and He had no problem with them; the only problem He had was the mind-set by which these people brought their offerings. Jesus praised the woman who brought all her livelihood; if this happened today, people would frown at the church and look upon the church as robbers of the poor. But Jesus, looking up, shows the direction where the offering was being honoured: Up to the Father, who watches the action of all men and who chooses to favour whomever He wishes to favour.

Prayer: My Father, I stand correct in all points before you. I receive grace from You in other to fully love You and the people You love so dearly. I desire deeply to spoil and lavish You with love in all I do today.

---

64 Hebrews 13:15
65 2 Corinthians 5:20
66 2 Corinthians 9:7
67 Luke 21:4
68 Luke 21:1

Righteousness Shows Us a God Who Lavished Us with All Gifts in Love

God gave His best in Jesus and lavished His Holy Spirit on us as a guarantee of more goodness to follow.[69]

He did not restrain Himself in any way when He thought about the creation of the world; rather, He poured more than enough resources into the earth for the use and livelihood of His man.

The essentials in our planet, like light, water, and air, are all in abundance. As we know, there is more water mass than land; no one can measure the air, and the light that comes from the solar system is indisputable in strength and resourcefulness compared to any source of light manufactured by man. But here is what the Bible says, in Jeremiah 10:13 and 51:16: *"Then He utters his voice. There is a multitude of water in the heavens,"* and *"He causes the vapours to ascend from the ends of the earth; He makes lightning for the rains; he brings the wind out of His treasure."*

These are powerful truths; God is the one who gives us all things to enjoy.[70] In Luke's gospel Jesus places our focus on a God who is always willing to give to us in abundance. Jesus said, *"Give and it shall be given to you: good measure, pressed down, shaking*

---

69   Ephesians 1:13–14
70   1 Timothy 6:17

together, and running over will be put into your bosom. For the same measure that you use, it will be measured back to you."

God blesses us because He loves us so dearly, and He causes us to prosper not because we deserve these things but because of His love and the pleasure He gets in seeing us come into these good things.[71]

God carries along with Him a certain excess that we cannot understand, but we should not push Him away. Just like Peter, who fell on his knees and said to Jesus, *"Depart from me, for I am a sinful man, O Lord."*[72] Why did Peter feel this way? Obviously, he could not handle the abundance of blessings that Jesus had brought into his life.

It is the abundance of mercies in God that brings people into repentance; it is his abundance of love that drives out all fear in our lives; it is His abundance of grace that causes us to walk steady in world of faith; it is the anointing that was poured out in our hearts that sustains our glorious Hope of Glory.

Prayer: Lord, I receive your mercy, goodness, and abundance and thank you for Your exceeding great love gifts toward me and all those I love. I rest in You in Jesus's name.

---

71   Luke 5:8
72   Luke 5:8

Holiness is Spending Time in God's Word out of Love, not Obligation

Love is a reciprocal relationship. Demonstrating love is a conscious decision to understand the other person so much that pleasing them comes naturally. The love of God is the same. Taking time to understand God's word is an act of love. When reading any book, you and the author are stroking minds, interacting and communing in a common place of agreement in the said subject.

The author of the Holy Scripture is the Holy Spirit. Peter, writing to the churches scattered abroad, expounded, saying, *"Knowing <u>this first</u> that no prophecy of Scripture is of any private interpretation. For prophecy never came by the will of man, but holy men of God spoke as they were moved by the Holy Spirit."*[73] Therefore, by reading the Bible you know intimately the God of the universe and your Creator.

The word keeps one from sin. How? King David wrote, *"Your word have I hidden in my heart that I may not sin against you."*[74]

The word keeps you focused on Him: *"But we will give ourselves continually to prayer and the ministry of the word."*[75]

Prayer: Dear Father, I love You so much. Open my eyes today to see You. Expound Your word to me; let me know Your ways intimately. Lord, draw me   closer to You by Your word as You are cleansing me daily and teaching me Your precepts.

---

73   2 Peter 1:20–21
74   Psalms 119:11
75   Acts 6:4

Righteousness is God Spending Time with Us

God's intention from the beginning was to dwell with man. That is why from the beginning God gave man His own Spirit[76] so that man can have the same image as He does and they can enjoy a life full of fulfilment of the same interests. God went ahead and placed man in a garden He had prepared called Eden, a word meaning delight.[77] Here in this place of comfort and the ambience of the garden the Lord intended to spend quality time with His man, and God also walked in the evening to have a wonderful fellowship time with man He had created.

When man stepped away from God to do his own thing, God still came looking and was still interested in a relationship that He thought was still worth having. This quest went on to where the cross was, and finally He opened the way for humanity to have that relationship with Him again.[78]

By the shed blood of Jesus on the cross, God can come to dwell finally in all those who would believe in the Lord Jesus Christ. *"At that day you will know that I am in My father and you in me, and I in you."*[79] This experience is what is called the indwelling of the

---

76   Genesis 2:7
77   Genesis 2:8
78   Genesis 3:8
79   John 14:20

Father, the Son, and the Spirit in and within a believer: the state of being born again.

When He arose from the dead, Jesus was so anxious to pour out His spirit (the spirit of God) back into man. He breathed on them and declared, *"Receive the Holy Spirit."*

He also promised since then that He will never leave and forsake us,[80] so that our confidence will always find a place to rest in Him.

Prayer: Father, I receive the fullness of Your Spirit today. Breathe on me and fill me up to running over. Let Your joy overtake me today. Lord, I receive Your Holy Spirit.

---

80   Hebrews 13:5

Holiness is the Humility to Listen to God

In communication, listening is the act of understanding the heart of the matter at hand, not just the surface of what is being spoken. Holiness is that willingness to listen to the heart of God and the readiness to carry out His commands.

Namaan was a leprous commander of the Syrian Army in Biblical times. He was made whole when he listened to the heart of what was said to him by God, through His prophet Elisha.[81]

Samuel heard the Lord but was not sure what he heard, until the experienced Eli, who was the priest then, instructed him. Samuel's response this time when he heard the voice of God was, "Speak, for your servant hears."[82]

The disciples of Jesus in John, chapter two, listened to Jesus and the heart of what was being spoken, after the mother of Jesus warned them, saying, "Whatever He says to you, do it."

King David, through his willingness to receive from God, conditioned his hearing and listening skills in God. We draw this wisdom from David's own words: *"God has spoken to me once; Twice have I heard this that power belongs to God."*[83]

---

81   2 Kings 5:13–14
82   1 Samuel 3:10
83   Psalms 62:11

Jesus reiterates this when he declares, "My sheep know My voice and I know them and they follow Me."

Prayer: Lord, I set my ear to hear You today. Speak, Lord, for by word I am healed and delivered. Open my ears to understand Your command, dear Lord, as You continue to prosper Your word in my life.

Righteousness is God Who Listens to Us All the Time

God hears you all the time. Our mind may not agree with this thought, because we have always expected God to do stuff when we need Him, not understanding that God wants a relationship from us, instead of a one-time miracle.

In Isaiah, God speaks about His glorious new covenant with the world, a period you and I are now enjoying. It is a period which the Lord describes through His prophet Jeremiah as a period of a general God-awareness in the hearts and minds of all mankind. *"No man shall teach his neighbour, and every man his brother, saying, know the Lord, for they shall know Me, from the least of them to the greatest of them, says the Lord. For I will forgive their iniquity, and their sin I will remember no more."*[84]

This was fulfilled when Jesus went to the cross; now everybody in the world is forgiven. So why are people still not experiencing God in their lives? Well, because they have to agree with this new deal. They have to sign up for this new contract to live for Jesus and allow Him to cleanse their heart and mind from that old way of thinking and reasoning.

There is always urgency in God to listen to us. Through Jeremiah His prophet, God draws our attention: *"Call to Me and I will*

---

84   Jeremiah 31:34

answer you, and show you great and mighty things, which you do not know."[85] This is God confirming His nearness to you when you pray, and describing His ability to meet you at the point of your need, and to even give you above the things that you ask of Him.

Jesus, who is the author and the finisher of our faith, demonstrated this relationship at the tomb of Lazarus when He looked up into heaven and prayed, "Father, I thank you that you have heard Me." Then He went on to say, *"And you always <u>hear</u> Me, but because of the people who are standing by I said this, that they may believe that You sent Me."*[86]

God calls himself I AM, showing His ever-present personality to save and to have fellowship with us. He hears us every time we call His name in the name of Jesus Christ.

Prayer: Thank You, Lord, for Your presence here today. I revere You, Lord, and I praise You for choosing me to be Yours. Help me today and reveal Yourself to me in a brighter way. Thank You, Jesus!

---

85   Jeremiah 33:3
86   John 11:41–42

Holiness is Speaking the Truth in Love

Holiness is an integral concept. This means that for a person to fully grasp holiness, they must see holiness as an integral matter, where the inside or the heart of a person matches his outward deeds.

A lot of us know that being holy means being set apart from the worldly way of thinking and acting, and instead using God's way of doing things. Yet many fail to realise that their intention must align properly with their new nature, which is in God.

The reason why we say God is holy is simply because God's inner and outward being match, and are one and the same. There is no difference between what God thinks, feels, and does. God is totally integral, and so the Bible tells us to be holy, for our God is a holy God.

Now, God is love, as the Bible points out, and His spirit is called the spirit of truth.[87] Therefore, a believer must allow these two natures of God to flow through them no matter what. Speaking the truth can be a difficult thing on occasion, but where it is spoken in love,[88] it will do what God does. It will bring healing, restoration, and harmony.

The apostle Paul encouraged the church at Colossi, *"Let your speech always be with grace, seasoned with salt, that you may know how you ought to answer each one."*[89]

---

87 John 16:13
88 Ephesians 4:15
89 Colossians 4:6

Prayer: Father, restore me in this area, Lord. Teach me today how to bring healing to the world through my inner and outer life. I surrender my tongue as a healing agent for You, Father. I celebrate this victory!

34

Righteousness is God Who Spoke and Is Still Speaking and will Speak

The righteousness of God speaks. When it speaks, it enforces change; it bring forth results; it heals and restores. But God intends to speak to us and through us.

Isaiah declared, *"I have not spoken in secret, in dark places of the earth; I did not say to the seed of Jacob, 'Seek Me in vain'; I, the LORD, speak righteousness, I declare things that are right."*[90]

So God in this verse says that He loves to speak plainly and not in secret, and when He does speak, He does so with righteousness.

It is His righteousness that believers should allow to speak through them, because He now resides in us. Paul points out that the righteousness of God speaks,[91] and it is effective and powerful when we start speaking in the righteousness of God.

But the righteousness of faith speaks in this way: Do not say in your heart, "Who will ascend into heaven?" (that is, to bring Christ down from above) or "Who will descend into the abyss?" Rather, what does it say? "The word is near you, in your mouth and in your heart." (That is, the word of faith which we preach.)[92]

Is He still speaking? Sure. The Bible says that God, who at various times and in various ways spoke in times past to the fathers by the prophets, has in these days spoken to us by His Son, whom He

---

90   Isaiah 45:19
91   Romans 10:6a
92   Romans 10:6–8

has appointed heir of all things, and through whom also He made the worlds.[93] He is still speaking through His Son. How? The Bible is your gateway to experiencing His Son, because Jesus is the word of God made flesh and dwelt among us[94] and now, He has left His spirit on earth to guide us and speak to us everything we need to know about Jesus.[95]

Prayer: Speak to me, Lord, for I am listening. My heart is ready for You and I ask that You make clear to me Your intentions at all times.

---

93   Hebrews 1:1–2
94   John 1:1. 14.
95   John 16:14

Holiness is a Willingness to Act for God in Love

Act today in love, not out of duress of any kind. For God, holiness is willingness to work in the Kingdom. Sometimes we see only the God part of the picture of the relationship. This is especially so in this day and age of self-gratification, exclusivity, and the promotion of self-independence, where people are full of themselves, forgetting that no man is an island and that everybody needs some other person to complete them.

God is looking for an individual who can willingly give himself up for His cause. Paul the apostle gave up everything to follow the call on his life. He said, *"Brethren, I do not count myself to have apprehended; but one thing I do, forgetting those things that are behind and reaching forward to those things which are ahead, I press toward the goal for the prize of the upward calling of God in Christ Jesus."*[96]

Holiness is that which apprehends one's heart in such a way that they are willing to carry it out in this world. Jesus gave Himself up to act out the will of God on the earth. The scripture says, *"Let this mind be in you which is also in Christ Jesus who, being in form of God, did not consider it robbery to be equal with God, made himself of no reputation, taking the form of a bondservant, and coming in the form of man."*[97]

---

96   Philippians 3:13–14
97   Philippians 2:5–7

What are we doing right now that every interest is God's, and we are in no way independently motivated? There needs to be a, *"Here I am, Lord, use me or send me,"* in the heart of every believer, and this not just casual rhetoric, but a deep and sincere longing to do anything for Him.[98]

Prayer: Lord, use me now for Your own glory, at Your own timing, and for Your own agenda, to the praise of Your name, Amen.

---

98   Isaiah 6:8

Righteousness is God Who is Love (in Action)

The scripture shows us a God who does not just act in love, behave in love or pour out love. Rather, God is love.

1 John 4:8 declares, *"He who does not Love does not know God, for God is love."*

Therefore, righteousness is the force of love or God in action. Without love, faith cannot work. For in Christ, the Bible says, *"Neither circumcision nor uncircumcision avail any thing, but faith working through Love."*[99]

So, all the great individuals of faith in Hebrews 11 became triumphant because of their understanding of the powerful workings of righteousness through a God who acts wholly in love because He is love.

The perfecting of love dispels every kind of fear in the life of man. *"There is no fear in Love, but perfect Love cast out all fear, because fear involves torment. But he who fears has not been made perfect in Love."*[100]

The actions of God and His works are not to terrify you; most of the time, it is to convict you in order to draw you closer for healing and restoration. When He acts, He brings life and hope. Jesus says, *"I have come that you may have life and that they may have it more abundantly."*[101]

---

99   Galatians 5:6
100   1 John 4:18
101   John 10:10

Love is what brought Jesus to the earth to die for us: *"As the Father Loved Me. I also loved you; abide in My love."* (John 15:9)

Love is what kept Him hanging on the cross: *"[Love] bears all things, believes all things hope all things, endures all things."* (1 Corinthians 13:7)

Love made Him lay down His life for many: *"Greater Love has no man than this, than to lay down one's life for His friends."* (John 15:13)

Love would raise us up to be with Jesus: *"Father, I desire that they also whom you gave me may be with Me where I am, that they may behold My glory which You loved Me before the foundation of the world."* (John 17:24)

Prayer: Father, I hunger to experience this righteousness in my life today. Move me in Your righteousness

Holiness is not When I Choose not to Sin – it is When I Choose to Love

1 Corinthians 13 depicts love in its full definition, development, and effect. To the believer, love should be the number-one motivation in everything we do. Why is holiness not choosing not to sin? It's because we are in a love world in Christ, a relationship full of love, so sin is not our consideration or our thought; we only think of the distribution of love.

Jesus describes the two pillars on which the whole of the commanded rest. Firstly, you shall love the Lord your God with all your soul, and with all your mind. Secondly, you shall love your neighbour as yourself. In essence, your choice to love is holiness, which means you are keeping the whole commandment.[102]

Jesus said, *"This is my commandment that we love one another, this is a charge to make a choice to Love, instead of trying not to sin." The secret is the choice to keep on loving your neighbour as yourself and the Lord as your Lord.*[103]

John the apostle declared boldly, *"He who does not Love does not know God, for God is Love. Why because this God who is Love dwells in you."*[104]

---

102   Matthew 22:37–40
103   John 15:14
104   1 John 4:8

Prayer: Father, give me the grace to walk in Your love and to rely on Your love and to come to know love intimately, deeply, and to embrace it fully in my life.

Righteousness is a God Whose Being is Love

The scripture says, *"For God so loved the world that He sent His only begotten Son, that whosoever believeth in Him should not perish but have eternal life."*[105]

God chose to love us just the way we are. How? By giving us Himself. This was a clear choice. The word says God is love.[106] It is so wonderful to know that love chose us, as opposed to many who may have imagined otherwise. It is this choice of love that manifests His righteousness towards us.

Love chose you. He is not trying to love us, or to become love to us, but He is love. This means that when we say love, we are actually saying God, the very essence of the love we feel and receive from Him.

It is love that saved us; it is love that called us children;[107] it is love that held Him on that tree. So righteousness is the power that demonstrates this great love of God.

Prayer: Dear Father, let me be a true reflection of this great love. This is my desire, Lord, that all may experience Your love through me.

---

105   John 3:16
106   1 John 4:8
107   1 John 3:1

Holiness is not Achievable by Strength

As a believer, Christ has made you holy, which is the reason you are reading this book—to let you know your present state. You may not look like it, but it is true: Christ makes every believer holy.

The Bible says, *"You are a holy nation."* That means, as sure as you cannot deny your earthly nationality and its characteristics, your spiritual nation is holy and its characteristic is holiness.

Again, the Bible says, *"And you, who once were alienated and enemies in your mind by the wicked works, yet now He has reconciled in the body of His flesh through death, to present you holy, and blameless, and above reproach in His sight."*[108] Those are the characteristics of your present state: holy, blameless, and beyond reproach.

So this is not by your works but what the Lord has done.[109] Use the word of righteousness and align yourself with it; then you will be able to discern what is good and evil and you will begin to line up with the Holy you God has made.

We cannot go out with our strength to try to work out holiness.[110] The experience with the power of holiness starts from your acceptance that God has made you holy; that despite your past, God says you are holy. When this happens in your heart, then the power of the holiness of God will become evident in your life.

---

108   Colossians 1:21–22
109   Philippians 1:6
110   1 Samuel 2:9

Prayer: Father, I totally submit to your word. I submit in my heart, mind, and will to admit my holy life in You. I go on from here with full assurance and peace in You.

Righteousness is the Strength of God's Love in Action

God is love, and because of this love the Bible says He is Good and His mercies endure forever. The flow of love is what righteousness is, and when righteousness starts to flow, the Bible says it delivers. *"Treasure of wickedness profits nothing, but righteousness delivers from death."*[111] No matter what deadness you are facing, His love sends righteousness your way today to deliver you!

Righteousness also tends you to life. You may be concerned where in life's way is the right, or perhaps things around you seem to be shaky or dead. His love has sent forth righteousness, and life is coming your way now in Jesus's name! The Bible says, *"As righteousness leads to life, so is he who pursue evil it to his own death."* It is amazing to know that righteousness is God's power to bring to life.

Righteousness watches and grows your seed. The scripture says that *"righteousness remains in the fruitful fields and the work of righteousness is quietness and assurance forever."*[112] So righteousness makes your God-given seed grow and gives you peace of mind in a troubled world. Righteousness can, in the worst situations, work out amazing results. You can see that it is judgment that works in dry and unfruitful places, in contrast to the fruitful places in

---

111   Proverbs 10:2; 11:19
112   Isaiah 32:16–18

life where righteousness fertilizes and grows out the best individuals who would believe.

Righteousness is God's love in action! We meditated a while ago that righteousness speaks, and now we read that righteousness will also work. Meditate deeply on this, and pray today to encounter the force of righteousness.

Prayer: Father, I receive the works of righteousness today in my life. I praise You for it!

Holiness is Submission to God's Word Because of Love

How submissive to the word of God are you? Remember that Jesus said, *"If you Love me, keep my commandment"*;[113] in essence, He said, "Keep my word." Holiness is submitting to the authority of God's word.

Holiness is desiring the word more than anything in the world. Paul describes his submission when he says, *"That I may know Him and the power of His resurrection, and the fellowship of His suffering, being conformed to His death."*[114] This stresses the mind to go all the way with and to desire His word. Job declares, *"I have not departed from the commandment of His lips; I have treasured the word of His mouth more than my necessary food."*[115]

King David describes his drive to know God as being like that of the deer that is in great need for water to quench her thirst. He says, *"As the deer pants for the water brooks, so pants my soul for you, oh God."*[116]

Secondly, King David displays his love for the word of God, and the place of purity and holiness in God's word as he praises God: *"Your word is very pure; therefore your servant loves it."*[117] It is this kind of love and not the dead, uninterested feeling but a

---

113   John 15:14
114   Philippians 3:10
115   Job 23:12
116   Psalms 42:1
117   Psalms 119:140

red-hot excitement to encounter God's righteousness through His word and to yield to its demands.

Like King David, we need a place of love in our hearts for the word in our time so that men can perceive our holiness the way God intended. As you submit to the word in love, God's righteousness will work massively in all your affairs. *"Oh, that you had listened to my commands! Then you would have had peace flowing like a gentle river and righteousness rolling over you like waves in the sea."*[118]

Prayer: Father, birth in me a deeper love to become submissive to your loving word, in Jesus's name.

---

118   Isaiah 48:18NLT

Righteousness is Christ Who Submitted Himself to Death but is Now Exalted, All in Love

The King of Glory came to die for His people, so they can have access to enter into life eternal, but to do this He had to humble himself and take on the guise of man and flesh, and even go to the cross. But God did not let Him remain there; He lifted Him and gave Him a name above all names.[119]

Righteousness is seen in the humility of Jesus. How Jesus submitted to God's word concerning the salvation of the souls of men[120]. God's plan was gory; it would be impossible; it demanded all of Jesus's life—and to make matters even more complicated, men will still not believe that it was done for them. But righteousness was being put on display in the submission of Jesus on the cross.

"Father, if you are willing, please take this cup of suffering away from me. Yet I want your will to be done, not mine. "Luke 22:44NLT

The book to the Hebrews encourages *"looking unto Jesus the author and finisher of our faith, who for the joy that was set before Him, endured the cross, despising the shame, and has sat down at the right hand of the throne of God."*[121]

Paul pointed out how he is not ashamed of the gospel of Christ. Why? Because talking about a King who would allow Himself

---

119   Philippians 2:6–11
120   Philippians 2:5-8NLT
121   Hebrews 12:2

to be hung on a cross seemed like weakness and foolishness to the Romans, who saw greatness in an emperor king and god, being the epitome of strength and valour. But Paul boldly declared, notwithstanding the Roman pre-supposition, *"I am not ashamed of the gospel of Christ."* Why? Paul says, *"For in it the righteousness of God is revealed from faith to faith, as it is written the just shall live by their faith."*[122]

Prayer: Father, I thank You for all You done for me through our Lord Jesus Christ. I believe the work of the cross and celebrate the work of righteousness

---

122   Romans 1:16–17

Holiness is Not of Law but of Love

It is truly by the workings of God that we can be holy; the scripture says, *"Therefore by the deeds of the law no flesh will be justified in His sight, for by the law is the knowledge of sin."*[123] Keeping a good religion and conduct of life can make no one holy. The love of God made us Holy.

So a reciprocal conduct of love is that which maintains this holy nature we have received from Him. The Bible specifies to *"put on the new man which was created according to God, in true righteousness and holiness."*[124]

Holiness cannot be attained by a family tree of Christian tradition and ceremonial ordination, but rather by genuine love to please God on relational terms.

Jesus said, *"If anyone loves me, he would keep my word,"*[125] not traditions. Notice He did not say "if anyone keeps my word" first, because HE knows that we must understand love before we can flow in obedience and submission; otherwise, your relationship with Him will be lacking life. Each day will not have that freshness or newness that comes with living faith, but instead the days are stale and sterile.

It is therefore love that should motivate while triggering actions—actions which comes deep from within your heart—to

---

123   Romans 3:20
124   Ephesians 4:24
125   John 14:23b

energize initiatives of worship, prayers, giving, and aiding. These are what enable us to do the works of God.

Prayer: Dear Father, I hunger for more of Your presence. As I meditate, fill me with the realities of righteousness and holiness today.

Righteousness Enforces God's Law

By love God has entrusted to us the Holy Spirit, who administers of righteousness *"and when He has come, He will convict the world of sin, and Righteousness and of Judgment."*[126] Oftentimes individuals going through trials will lean to the side of judgment; they will claim that God is teaching them a lesson for something they did. Where there is a place for this conclusion, as a believer there is something different working for you. In your case, the Lord, through His Spirit, ministers righteousness to you right in the middle of trials.

The Holy Spirit places righteousness in our hearts and hands to experience God and the ability to represent Him here on earth. Jesus said, *"All things that the Father has are Mine. Therefore I said that He will take of Mine and declare it to you."*[127]

Part of that declaration is a declaration of the legal framework of righteousness. Jesus expounded when He says in the same chapter, *"Of righteousness because I go to the Father and you see me no More."* This means His activities here are done but He would send to them the Holy Spirit, who is full of the fruits of all goodness and righteousness and truth.[128] Through Him the apostles and all who will believe will have the same authority He had on earth to do the things He did before their very eyes.

So, we are right to challenge the enemy whenever he comes

---

126   John 16:8
127   John 16:15
128   Ephesians 5:9

around, because he has been judged and you have been given God righteousness, which is based on unchanging promises and love of God, to command him out of your life. Righteousness is God enforcing His righteous laws to ensure the victory of the believer.

Holiness is the Precious Sacrifice We Give unto God

Praising and worshipping God are all precious and holy in the sight of God. Bringing offerings and tithings is making precious sacrifices before God.

David said, *"I will enter His gate with thanksgiving in his heart and His court with praise."*[129]

Holy people are people that are "made free"[130] by the works of Christ and so they are free to lift up holy hands toward Heaven and give God all the praise and adoration due to Him forever more.

Therefore, the knowledge of being holy is the greatest realization one can attain after salvation, because until that point, one has not come to terms with a whole lot of the benefits that lay in Christ, in God.

This awareness is an awesome sacrifice to God because you will enter a relationship full of praise and the glory of God.

Prayer: Father, I rejoice in holiness and holy living today. Oh! I will continue to press toward the mark for the prize of my high calling of God in Christ Jesus!

---

129   Psalms 100:1
130   Romans 8:3

Righteousness is God's Precious Gift to Us

Righteousness is that powerful gift God gave us through His son Jesus.

"For if by the one man's offence death reign by one, much more those who receive abundance of grace and of the gift of righteousness will reign in life through the one Jesus Christ."[131] Righteousness is this precious gift, which give back the power to mankind to govern their affairs of this life once again. As it were, mankind fell from the grace of God[132] but the gift of righteousness picked mankind back up and set man again on solid grounds of faith in Christ.

"Therefore, as through one man's offense judgment came to all men, resulting in condemnation, even so through one Man's righteous act the free gift came to all men, resulting in justification of life."[133]

Righteousness is that free gift which resulted in our justification—justification which is wholly from the consequence of sin and death. We are no longer plagued by the guilt of errors made in the past, even those which have their roots in the inheritance of frail and cursed humanity.

Look at the reason why we know the righteousness of God. The Bible says, *"Therefore, if anyone be in Christ, he is a new creation; old things are passed away; behold, all things have become*

---

131   Romans 5:17
132   Romans 3:23
133   Romans 5:18 NKJV

new."[134] We are made anew by His righteousness and we possess every quality as God's own righteousness.

Righteousness is the gift which comes upon the man who accepts Jesus Christ as Lord and saviour. This transforming power of Almighty God transforms the person into a new creation and makes the person the righteousness of God. *"For He made Him who knew no sin to be sin for us, that we might become the righteousness of God in Him."*[135]

Furthermore, it is very interesting to experience your new wardrobe. This gift of righteousness is the robe of God. In the natural it will be like getting someone the perfect and permanent fit of a suit or dress. Righteousness is the perfect fit for mankind. **Refer Isaiah 61:10**

Prayer: Father, I receive all that You have for me. No eye has seen nor ear has heard nor has it entered the mind of man what you have for us. But Lord, by faith I stand to receive all today.

---

134   1 Corinthians 5:17
135   2 Corinthians 5:21 NKJV

Holiness is a Mind Set on God in Love

Our mind is the central processing unit (CPU) of the body. We receive revelation via the spirit, understand it with our mind, and act it out within the body.

The middleman is the mind, and a mind stayed on God is that holy mind that understands clearly what the spirit is saying. A mind set on God can never walk contrary to the plan of God.

Minds set on God receive the peace of God.[136]

A mind set on Him will never lack revelation[137] and success will attend everything he touches.[138] Minds set on God cannot suffer from unbelief.

God is pleased when our minds ask Him for direction all the time, for He is our Lord. We need to study the concept of lordship intensely and we would perceive more of the ministry of the Holy Spirit when Jesus said of Him that He would "guide you into all truth." Like an orchestral conductor, He will lead you into the right things and we must follow, if we desire to be fulfilled.

Apostle Peter encouraged through the Holy Spirit, *"Therefore gird the loins of your mind, be sober, and rest your hope fully upon the grace that is to be brought to you at the revelation of Jesus Christ."*[139]

Holiness is the mind that is set on and is resting fully in the

---

136   Isaiah 26:3
137   Psalms 119:130
138   Joshua 1:8
139   1 Peter 1:13

grace of God. That mind is rested and calm in this life. When the storms rage and the billows roll, the mind set on God in love says all is well.

Prayer: Father, I thank You for Your desire to see me excel in my mind and today I respond to Your call. I commit to keep my mind conducive to Your presence at all times, help me, Lord.

Righteousness is God's Mind-set about Us

od made up his mind about us a long time ago and He declared it in His word. He says, *"For I know the thought I think toward you, says the Lord, thoughts of peace and not of evil, to give you a future and a hope."*[140] Jesus is the righteous mind of God in action. Jesus came to declare the mind of God in all His deeds and teachings.[141]

Man cannot fathom God's thoughts, even if God allows him to see them, His thoughts are vast and enormous and the only thing we can do is to raise our heart up and say, "Lord, I receive them." Because of His wondrous love for us the psalmist had to ask the Lord, *"What is man that you are mindful of him?"*[142]

God's mind is full of His thoughts and intent for man. No doubt God has prepared so much for His man. The Bible reveals, *"No eye has seen, nor ear heard, nor has it entered the heart of man the things which God has prepared for those who love Him."*[143] This is one scripture that lights my fire. Let us reflect on the first man, Adam. Before God made Him, God had finished and made all provisions Adam's body, soul, and spirit would ever require to live a whole and healthy life. To date, God has not changed any of those provisions; they still work perfectly when put to the test. God is amazing.

---

140 Jeremiah 29:11

141 Act 1:1 / 1 Corinthians 1:24

142 Psalms 8:4

143 1 Corinthians 2:9

When speaking to the prophet Jeremiah, God said, *"You have seen well, for I am ready to perform My word."*[144] In Isaiah, God spoke concerning how mindful He is to perform His good word in our lives. He said, *"So shall my word be that goes forth from My mouth; it shall not return to me void, but it shall accomplish what I please, and it shall prosper in the thing for the which I sent it."*[145]

God's mind is set for good on the people of God, to perform His word which you have received, because concerning His covenant, He said He will ever be mindful of His covenant.[146] Adam needed to have an open eye to see it, but he missed it. Thank God we have Jesus Christ, the Last Adam, who saw and kept God's promise.[147]

The scriptures declare, even in all these, that the stamp of approval is still on all God's promises, which He intends to carry out in your life. *"For all the promises of God in Him are yes, and in Him are Amen, to the glory of God through us."*[148]

Prayer: My Father, I am glad You are revealing great secrets to me for Your glory. Open my eyes even more so I may truly see the things You desire for me. I thank You for giving me this desire toward Your great covenants.

---

144   Jeremiah 1:12
145   Isaiah 55:11
146   Psalms 89:34
147   1 Corinthians 15:45 / Hebrews 12:2
148   2 Corinthians 1:20

Holiness is Wholeness in God

Wholeness is a unique word when read in the Hebrew. It is from the root word *shalom*, meaning peace, prosperity, wholeness, and a state of wellbeing. Holiness is the awareness of these dimensions in God and walking in them.

Holiness is the oneness that we are partakers of the divine nature. God is called Jehovah Shalom, meaning, "God our peace, our wholeness." In response to having peace and reliance on God, we are walking in holiness. *"And let the peace of God rule your hearts, to which also you were called in one body; and be thankful."*[149]

Wholeness brings the thought of the whole of man in the place of transparent worship before God, to be preserved by God for the day of the Lord, which on its own is wholeness. *"Now may the God of peace Himself sanctify you completely; and may your whole spirit, soul and body be preserved blameless at the coming of the Lord Jesus Christ."*[150]

Prayer: I declare my wholeness today in Jesus's name. I confess Your word in Colossians that says I am complete in Christ Jesus. I walk consistently today in this revelation and Father, I thank You today for the power never to waver in this.

---

149   Colossians 3:15
150   1 Thessalonian 5:23

Righteousness is God Becoming One with Us

The Bible reveals how God came into the world when *"His word became flesh and dwelt among us and we behold His Glory, the glory as of the only begotten son full of grace and truth, this in the person of our Lord and saviour Jesus Christ."*[151]

This merger of divinity and humanity is the power of righteousness in action; it was God becoming one with humanity and humanity becoming one with divinity. Jesus's prayer for all believers was this: *"I in them. And You in me; that they may be perfect in one, and that the world may know that You have sent Me, and have loved them as You have loved Me."*[152]

The force of righteousness is binding divinity to the human spirit. Which other creation can experience such a merger without losing all quality of their being but righteousness, that in this great merge we enjoy our uniqueness yet being one with God?

Righteousness is the God-life which flows from within the believer to reach this dying world. It is the power of God that is working effectively[153] in us as believers to will and to do according to His good pleasures,[154] as the scripture reveals to us.

---

151   John 1:14
152   John 17:23
153   1 Thessalonians 2:13
154   Philippians 2:13

Prayer: Father, I celebrate Your life in me and I sincerely call on Your name today that I may not receive Your wonderful life in vain. Use me for Your glory.

Holiness Ascends

Peter, by the Holy Spirit, wrote to the saints urging us to be holy because God is a holy God.[155] So, our holiness is unto God, not so much as unto man or establishments. One can earn the position as the most reputable saint in their church circle or the servant of the year, but that form of holiness may simply be toward men or leadership. Holiness ascends. It is directed to the holy things of God. It grows up, it matures, and it bears holy fruits.

The apostle Paul points out and pleads with the saints at Rome, *"I beseech you therefore brethren, by the mercies of God, that you present your bodies a living sacrifice, holy and acceptable to God, which is your reasonable service."*

Being holy, therefore, is allowing holy worship to rise unto God from your heart in the form of your daily conduct, your core values, and your manner of life. Paul, by the Holy Spirit, instructs, *"And whatever you do, do it heartily, as to the Lord and not to men."*[156]

Again, Paul declares, *"I desire therefore that the men pray everywhere, lifting up holy hands, without wrath and doubting."*[157]

'Hands,' one might want to say, refers to physical hands, but 'hand' denotes works of one's hands, because it follows with doing so without wrath and doubting. Ascending holiness is Abel's sacrifice, breaking the barrier of a cursed sky from earth and ascending to the delight of the Father.

Since you and I have received this newness of life, even now

---

155   1 Peter 1:16
156   Colossians 3:23 NKJV
157   1 Timothy 2:8

our life needs to be positioned as that ascending body, as Christ who, after death, wanted nobody to touch Him until He had risen up to heaven to see the Father. Even so we must live our lives free from the touch of the world at all times.

Holiness is ascending worship, a life full of gratitude and being willing at all times to honour God by the good works of the spirit, mind, and hands.[158] The Bible declares, *"You also, as living stones, are being built up a spiritual house, a holy priesthood, to offer up sacrifices acceptable to God through Jesus Christ."*[159]

Prayer: Father, I pray today that the words of my mouth and the meditations of my heart be acceptable in Your sight. I receive Your wisdom to direct my heart in all my service to You. Equip me to also become a light for others who desire true worship in Jesus's name.

---

158   Titus 2:7
159   1 Peter 2:5

Righteousness Descended

Through the spirit of God the prophet Jeremiah gave the oracle of God in this manner: *"Behold the days are coming,' says the Lord, 'that I will raise to David a branch of Righteousness; a king shall reign and prosper, and execute judgment and righteousness in the earth. In His days Judah will be saved. And Israel will dwell safely; now this is His name by which He will be called: THE LORD OUR RIGHTEOUSNESS."*[160]

God declared that His righteousness was what mankind needed to be free from the grip of sin. As the Bible declares, *"But when the fullness of time had come, God sent forth His Son, born of a woman, born under the Law, to redeem those who were under the law, that we might receive the adoption as sons."*[161]

This is why the apostle points out about Jesus, *"For what the Law could not do in that it was weak through the flesh, God did by sending His Son in the likeness of flesh on account of sin: He condemn sin in the flesh, that the righteous requirements of the law might be fulfilled in us who do not walk according to the flesh but according to the spirit."*[162]

These are glorious scriptures pointing to the mighty work of descending righteousness. Descending righteousness means God destroying the works of darkness in the lives of man and establishing a new way of life which is the freedom in Christ Jesus.

---

160   Jeremiah 23:5–6
161   Galatians 4:1–4
162   Romans 8:3–4

Jesus says, *"Therefore if the Son makes you free, you shall be free indeed."*[163]

Prayer: Lord, I am ever grateful that all You are, You gave to me in righteousness. Lord, I receive You as my righteousness even today and I connect readily its full authority upon my life even now in Jesus's name. Thank You, Lord, I receive the fullness of it now.

---

163   John 8:36

Holiness is to Understand Our Weaknesses and Share Them to God in Love

After a time weakness, when kept too close, kills. When we mention the word 'holy' we must understand that it means a life where the interior of your being matches your exterior words and actions. The interior in the believers will mean "Christ in you, the Hope of Glory."[164] The Bible says that without holiness no man sees God, and most of us attribute this statement to our life in deeds; where this is right, one must not forget that God needs us to be fully exposed to Him. Regarding things that are laid deep within, the deepest hurt or secrets and places no man can reach, these can become areas that may end up being a foothold[165] for the enemy of your soul, as the scripture stresses. Hence, being holy is also the willingness to bring those things into the forefront where you and God can deal with them.

Yes, a lot of us would say that God knows everything. Listen to David's confession:

"...Have mercy upon me, O God, According to Your loving kindness; According to the multitude of Your tender mercies, Blot out my transgressions.

---

164   Colossians 1:27b
165   Ephesians 4:27

[2] *Wash me thoroughly from my iniquity, And cleanse me from my sin.*

[3] *For I acknowledge my transgressions, And my sin is always before me.*

[4] *Against You, You only, have I sinned, And done this evil in Your sight That You may be found just when You speak, And blameless when You judge."*[166]

In this part of the scripture I am sure David spoke it as he penned it down and poured out his heart before God. We must also realize the power of presumptuous sins.[167] We think it is OK to continue in sin and God is all right with it for now, but David, having realized his weakness, pleaded, "Let them not have dominion over me."

Prayer: God, remove every presumptuousness from my heart and mind and help me to overcome weaknesses before they become sin in my life.

---

166   Psalms 51:1–4
167   Psalms 19:13

Righteousness is the Cleansing Agent of God on Our Shortcomings and Failures

In his time of sickness and disease, Job had several advisers who counselled him. Job was not willing to hear them because he claimed that he was righteous, and that God had His plans and explanations for why things are the way they are.

One of these advisors spoke concerning the righteousness of man. He said, "How can a man be righteous before God? Or how can he be pure who is born of a woman?"[168]

These are questions that people still ask today, but thank God they were answered over two thousand years ago when Jesus Christ, through His death, burial, and resurrection, became our wisdom, righteousness, sanctification, and redemption.

Paul declared through the Holy Spirit, *"For He made Him who knew no sin to be sin for us, that we might become the righteousness of God."*[169]

Every person who accepts Jesus Christ as Lord and saviour and lives his or her life according to the love of God must be in peace because you are the righteousness of God. This righteousness is the power of God to declare and make the vilest sinner or the most pretentious saint as white as snow. The believer will have

---

168   Job 25:4
169   1 Corinthians 1:30

no sense and effect of any wrongdoing,[170] as long as they live on this side of eternity. This is marvellous!

Prayer: I celebrate the freedom and cleansing that came because of Your righteousness.

---

170   Hebrews 10:2

Holiness is a Burning Desire to See God

The one desire of the holy man is to be with the holy God whom he or she shares holiness from. The scripture declares that all God wants to see by His many correction and dealing with the believer is that "we might become sharers in His holiness.[171] If this is God's burning desire, then the believer must also burn eternally in the same passion.

Moses's desire was to see God, when he said to God, "Please show me your glory."[172] We are to desire to see God's glory even in our day, even more so as we see the days come to an end. Holiness is reaching upward to God to be even closer to Him. In the end, our goal is to make Heaven, to hear God's great voice of welcome.[173] We are to desire to also see others receive their crown of righteousness.[174] These are all great and worthy desires of your holy calling!

Paul the apostle shared with us his burning heart's desire to see the Lord in these compelling lines: *"Finally, there is laid up for me the crown of righteousness, which the Lord, the righteous Judge, will give to me on that Day, and not to me only but also to all who have loved His appearing."* To further enlighten us, Paul tells us about how he determined to pursue this worthy ambition: *"I press*

---

171   Hebrew 12:10bAMP
172   Exodus 33:18
173   Matthew 25:21
174   2 Timothy 4:8

toward the goals for the prize of the upward call of God in Christ Jesus."[175]

As believers we must be under observation and keep the premise of the horizontal calling and the vertical calling alive. Horizontal calling is the commission of God to be witnesses, workers in the vineyard, and those who are to take charge[176] here on earth until Jesus comes. On the other hand, we must not forget to look up[177] all so very often, to give God praise for things He has done and the promises He has kept, and to worship in spirit and in truth.[178]

Prayer: Father, I am grateful that You have called me. I remain thankful that this desire that You have laid in my heart is from You. Lord, let it remain rich towards You.

---

175   Philippians 3:14
176   Luke 19:13
177   Luke 21:28
178   John 4:24

Righteousness is God Who Desires Fellowship with Man

After the Garden of Eden, apparently where man failed and first made his choice to live without God by wanting to run the affairs of earth alone, God still came looking for man in the cool of the day.

God did not stop there, but continued to pursue man and to bring man out of the mess he was in. When Jesus came down to earth, His great mission statement was, *"The Son of man came to seek and save that which was lost."*[179]

God still seeks, even today, men and women alike that will come into fellowship with Him. This is an awesome privilege that God seeks man for fellowship.[180] The reason must be clear: He wants to save man from destruction, and by relating to God, He shows us the true cause of events around us and guides us to the safe path.[181]

God seeks man for fellowship because there is a place in every man, which God has embedded into man, that calls and cries to God involuntarily; there is that instinct to call on God in times of deep distress.[182] This is the reason He said, *"Call to Me and I will*

---

179 Luke 19:10

180 1 Corinthians 1:9

181 Isaiah 30:21

182 Psalms 34:6

answer and show you great and mighty things that you know noth-ing of."[183]

Prayer: Father, I call out for earnest fellowship with Your Holy Spirit today, as I wait in great expectation for Your coming.

---

183   Jeremiah 33:3

Holiness Raises Up in Love in the Face of Temptation

Holiness is the one power to stand in times of trouble. Holiness enables you to lift your hands boldly to God for answers to prayers. Holiness is integral, which means your life, in your inner being, corresponds with the life you're living. When that is the case, it becomes very difficult for temptation to alight or have a grip on your soul.

Holiness is the power against the scrutiny of the eye of the heathen world.[184] As they look to persecute you, they will find only holiness, which is from God, and their mouths will be shut. Holiness brings to the believer's heart this unusual boldness and testimony in time of trials and temptations to uphold them and bring them victory.[185] They will glorify God.

Holiness prepares you to forgive easily and not be tempted to hold grudges and malice against anybody. *"Let all bitterness, wrath, anger, clamour, and evil speaking be put away from you, with all malice ad be kind to one another, tender-hearted, forgiving one another, even as God in Christ forgave you."*[186]

Prayer: Father, I stand boldly in my confession of holiness towards You and my commitment to enforce all my righteousness privileges in You, in Jesus's name.

---

184   Philippians 2:15AMP
185   Proverbs 28:1 NKJV
186   Ephesians 4:31–32

Righteousness is God Raising Up a Standard Against the Enemy

Our daily battle is fashioned in a way whereby when they attack us, we are so incapable of handling them. Paul expresses the kind of battle we are faced with everyday: *"For we wrestle not against flesh and blood but against principalities, against powers, against ruler of the darkness of this age, against spiritual wickedness in the heavenly places."*[187]

Against these forces we as humans stand no chance, but this is our assurance that when the enemy comes in like a flood, the spirit of the Lord will lift up a standard against him.[188]

The spirit of the Lord is the redeeming Lord who has declared to us who believe that His is our righteousness. The arm of righteousness fights for us in the unseen realm to foil all attacks of the evil one.[189]

Therefore, the fight with guilt and the shame of the past can no longer find a place to come against you. On your course to do great things for God in Christ, the enemy would want to come in and begin to show you how unworthy you are, and how it is not possible to attain new levels of the word, purity, holiness, prayer life, business, career, and help.[190]

---

187   Ephesians 6:12
188   Isaiah 59:19b
189   Isaiah 59:16
190   2 Corinthians 1:9–10

At these times you depend on the righteousness of God,[191] which says that you are holy and strong in Christ, and which also says you have the word of faith right in your mouth to declare the things of God into your situation and they will come to pass. That is God raising a standard against the enemy.

Prayer: Father, I thank You because without You I cannot do anything. Thanks for Your great love towards me. I thank You for every victory won and I will give You all the glory for future blessings.

---

191   Romans 10:8

Holiness is Lifting God Up in Our Lives

Holiness is the evidence that the world looks for to determine if God lives on earth. Our lives of wholeness in God and purity are powerful tools for God to elevate His work in our lives.

Holiness is a phenomenal force, even stronger than natural forces. The early church literally turned nations upside down; even the well-trained army of the Roman Empire could not withstand the force of holy men. Concerning the ministry of the early church and the effect, this was an eyewitness account: *"But when the did not find them, they dragged Jason and some brethren to the rulers of the city, crying out, these who have turned the world upside down have come here too."*[192]

Why? Because holy men are usable instruments of the Holy Spirit. They are subservient to the works and leadings of the Holy Spirit. The scripture declares, *"Knowing that first, no prophecy of scripture is of any private interpretation, for prophecy never came by the will of man, but holy men of God spoke as they were moved by the Holy Spirit."*[193]

Holy men are the lifters of God upon the earth; as a result of holy living, eventually the glory of God will be revealed. So the scriptures encourage thus: *"And let us not grow weary in while doing well, for in due season you shall reap when you do not lose heart."*[194] We are led by the Holy Spirit when holiness is that genuine

---

192   Act 17:6
193   1 Peter 1:20–21
194   Galatians 6:9

Christlike nature that man hungers to attain. The Lord also expects us to be holy so that our lives will be lifted.

Prayer: Father, I submit to Your mighty plan to lift Your name high in the earth. Use me in any way that You deem fit. I rejoice in Your choice.

Righteousness is an Exalter of Any People

The wise man Solomon reveals the secret to the ultimate success of any nation, people, or family. He says, *"Righteousness exalts a nation, but sin is a reproach to any people."*

Around the world today governments seek answers to the growing problem of terrorism, genocide, wars, and all sorts of evil lurking at the doorsteps of nations, and so far they have had no real solution. Righteousness here, the Bible says, exalts a nation. The strength of a nation, however, is determined by the moral strength and structure of its people and their family unit and the regard of the matrimonial institution of marriage.

Where morality declines, the sanity of the nation declines as well. An immoral individual will in the end become very incapable of living a moral life when the need arises. The nations of the world suffer from a problem that only the works of righteousness can solve.

A lot of regimes around the world that may have taken or toppled a corrupt government will stand and brag about their own policies and agenda, but along the line, they begin to perpetuate the crimes of their predecessors. This is simply because without righteousness man is futile and worthless and unable to take care of itself.

Solomon, arguably the richest man and the most influential ruler that has ever lived, did not arrogate his exalted throne to great wealth and power he attained; instead, he clearly referred his peers at the time to the righteousness of God. I believe the same in our day and age: in all governance and leadership this verdict must thunder down the hearts and minds of the nations that righteousness exalts a nation but sin is a reproach to any people.[195]

Religion is a form of righteousness; shamefully, it is not righteousness of God but of man. Every moral and spiritual invention of man has a depreciating value in the end, and so also 'his' governmental policies and system; it has life when it starts, but dies a shameful death in the end.

Hear the heart's desire of one who was an instrument used by God to spread good news of salvation throughout the known world of his time: *"Yet indeed I also count all thing loss for the excellence of the knowledge of Christ Jesus my Lord, for whom I have suffered the loss of all things, and count them as rubbish, that I may gain Christ, and be found in Him, not having my own righteousness, which is from the law, but that which is through faith in Christ, the righteousness whic1h is from God by Faith."*[196]

---

195   Proverbs 14:34
196   Philippians 3:8–9

Meditate on Scripture on Resting in God

I declare my rest in You: Matthew 11:28
I declare You are my righteousness: Jeremiah 23:6
I declare my rest in Your Spirit and not my own strength: Zachariah 4:6
I declare You are my peace: Ephesians 2:14 / John 14:27
I declare my completeness in You Lord: Colossians 2:10
I declare my trust in Your divine plan for me: 1 Corinthians 2:16
I declare Your wisdom is sufficient for me: 1 Corinthians 1:30
I declare my firm reliance on Your leading voice: Isaiah 30:21-22
I declare my rest in Your provision: Psalm 34:10
I declare that my solace comes from You: Mark 6:32-42
I declare my trust in Your active presence which goes with me: Exodus 33:14
I declare my mind is rested on You: Isaiah 26:3
I declare I shall not be alarmed: Philippians 1:28
I declare my trust on Your sure foundation to run my race and finish my course: Acts 20:24
I declare my comfort and joy in Your presence: Psalm 16:11
I declare my rest in Your counsel and help: John 14:16
I declare that I trust You through every season: Isaiah 43:19
I declare my rest in Your voice in times of frustration: Galatians 6:9
I declare that all things are working together for my good: Romans 8:28
I declare Your lordship over my life: John 20:28